Helen Bigelow Merriman

What Shall Make Us Whole?

Helen Bigelow Merriman

What Shall Make Us Whole?

ISBN/EAN: 9783337811983

Printed in Europe, USA, Canada, Australia, Japan

Cover: Foto ©Thomas Meinert / pixelio.de

More available books at **www.hansebooks.com**

WHAT SHALL MAKE US WHOLE?

OR

THOUGHTS IN THE DIRECTION OF MAN'S SPIRITUAL AND PHYSICAL INTEGRITY.

BY

HELEN BIGELOW MERRIMAN.

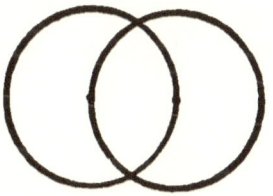

BOSTON:
CUPPLES AND HURD,
94 BOYLSTON STREET.
1888.

PREFATORY NOTE.

THIS essay was begun at the request of a few friends, and without any thought of book-making. Its appearance in the present form is not intended to claim for it either completeness or permanent value. It is at best but a rough and imperfect sketch of a spiritual possibility now coming into the field of human vision. It attempts only to fix a few points and establish a few relative values, in anticipation of the time when human research and experience shall complete the picture.

As the essence of a sketch is its grouping of details in order to handle them in their larger relations, so in this essay metaphysical terms are used with less regard to the distinctions between them than to their common aspect as expressing phases of the universal life.

INTRODUCTION.

WHAT SHALL MAKE US WHOLE?

—◆—

INTRODUCTION.

TWO men paint the same landscape. One of them sees first the details, — the flowers and rocks of the foreground, the cattle, the individual trees; these he represents one after another with painstaking fidelity, and is surprised to find that the sum of them does not make a satisfactory picture. The other notes first the contrast between land and sky; marks how the light falls broadly on the meadow, sweeps up one hillside, leav-

itual as well as the physical being of man,
and he will probably tell you that the spiritual is too vague an element to be ad-
mitted into his calculations in any practical
way. He agrees, perhaps, that man's mental and spiritual condition must affect his
physical health; but he feels that the spiritual realm is quite distinct from that in
which he labors, and that its laws, if it have
any, are too little understood to be relied
on in a practical emergency. And yet, if
God's will is the central controlling force
of the universe, which it must be if God
exists at all, man's relation to Him must
transcend and include all other relations
in which man stands, and must form not
only a factor, but *the prime factor* in all
life's problems. Any attempt to harmonize life's discordant elements must surely
fail of complete success so long as this
prime factor is left out. The physician
confesses this when he uncovers his head
to the mystery of life and death, and owns

that in this direction his art has limitations which he can never hope to transcend.

Meanwhile some plain people, not over-burdened with scientific knowledge, remembering the miracles and mystic sayings of Christ, deeply convinced of the reality of unseen things, have here and there cherished the belief that in some way disease can be routed by spiritual weapons, and man made in the end so perfectly whole in body and spirit that disintegration and death will have no hold upon him. To-day these theories are set forth in a more coherent form than ever before, under such names as " Mental Healing " or " Mind Cure," " Faith Cure," " Christian Science," etc.[1] Faith is the essential element in them all; but the more thoughtful class have,

---

[1] These are all different phases of the same movement. " Christian Science " tends to magnify the individual. " Faith Cure " relies on God, without making much effort to understand the methods of His working. " Mind Cure " holds a wise course between the two, and is by far the most promising for future usefulness.

as a result of their faith, discerned certain spiritual laws which give solidity to their work, and go far to justify them in claiming for the new practice the name of a spiritual science.

Faith leads us to turn towards something as yet unseen, but which we think may exist.   If the thing is really there, it becomes more and more apparent to us as we turn, so that gradually our faith is merged in belief and positive assurance.   The mental — or, better, spiritual — healers, starting with a profound faith that God is the great Reality, and that man, in virtue of his relation to God, is first and chiefly a spiritual being to be influenced most potently from the spiritual side, have had the courage of their convictions, and by surrendering themselves to this view of things and putting it into practice down to the smallest detail, they have achieved such success in healing as in the minds of many abundantly proves the rightness of their assumption, and transfers their practice from the uncertain realm of faith to the terra firma of established principles.

The advance they have made is thus an ethical, one might almost say biological, rather than a merely intellectual one. The propositions which the teachers of Mental Healing advance with unquestioning faith, and in unusual terminology, are none other than the deepest spiritual truths of Christianity. These truths are unfolding to man to-day in a thousand ways as never before, leading many persons to believe that we are on the verge of a new spiritual era, a blossoming of the whole age, a second coming of Christ in the hearts of his people. The special credit due to the Mind Cure is, that its disciples have dared to insist that these deepest spiritual truths shall become practical, operative, regnant, here and now.

This is, after all, the greatest service that can be done for mankind, — to bring truth out of the realm of the abstract, and incorporate it with daily life. It always requires great courage and faith to do this, and never more than now, when science has so exalted the truth of physical facts that spiritual truth, which often revolutionizes these facts, can scarcely get a hearing in some quarters.

If the Mind Cure really heals the sick, it will soon have followers enough, and win its way in spite of all opposition; but in these early days, when it is struggling for recognition, it needs a word to show that its basis is one on which all who recognize the spiritual life can agree. The Church should welcome it as helping men to realize God so practically in all things as to overcome the deep scepticism which haunts even the most spiritual lives. If it can be shown that God is so immediately present in man and in matter that He can be appealed to directly for all good ends; if His Spirit is a practical working force so close at hand that each of us may use it with confidence in the small as well as the large matters of daily life, on the sole condition of a rightness in such use, which is but another name for right-eousness, — if this can be proved true and brought home to the experience of men, it will do much to check the growth of materialism which now threatens to take on such alarming proportions.

Why do we say " it " and not " he," in speaking of the Spirit? Simply because the Church, although she has long taught the divine personality of the Spirit, has not succeeded in making man trust to its help in the smaller details of life. Rever-ence has held God at arm's length from His world. The present need is to make man conscious of the universality of Spirit; and to achieve this we lay aside the pro-noun " he " for the time being, though we do not relinquish the idea which the per-sonal pronoun implies, — for in man's liv-

ing and personal relation to the universal
Deity lies his hope of being made finally
whole.

The following pages are an attempt to
set forth in familiar terms the philosophy and practice of Mental Healing. It
should be said that although the names
" Mental Healing " and " Mind Cure " are in
such general use that it seems necessary
to employ them here, they are somewhat
misleading, because they give an impres-
sion that the cures are wrought either by
the influence of the mind over the body,
or by the influence of one human mind
over another; neither of which is wholly
true. The human mind — or better, spirit
— can achieve nothing that is good except
as that mind becomes the channel of the
infinite Spirit of God. As this truth is
more clearly recognized, we may hope that
the names now in use will give way to
more adequate ones, such as " Spiritual
Healing," " Spiritual Science," etc.

THE PHILOSOPHY OF MENTAL
HEALING.

THE PHILOSOPHY OF MENTAL HEALING.

THE philosophy of Mental Healing is the extremest idealism. Its leading propositions may be thus stated.

God, the only Reality, forever creates, from a necessity of His own being. The material universe, culminating in man and finding its true cause and explanation in him, is but an expression of God's thought. All created things below man move in blind obedience to God's will as we know it under the name of natural law. In man we find a being endowed with the power of choice, of dual action. He may turn away from material things to recognize and

believe in God, his source, or he may turn
away from God and believe in his own
foreshadowing, — that is, material things,
thereby endowing them with a delusive
appearance of reality.   Reality, in the last
analysis, is the underived power to produce
effects, and can be predicated only of God.
Man's mistaken choice, whether caused by
ignorance or self-will, his tendency to look
away from God and put confidence in material things, has been and is, the source
of all his sin and sickness.   The whole
duty imposed on man by God is the duty
of turning to and recognizing Him.   This
duty includes all others.   Failure to per-
form it produces disorder, which, if we
accept it, becomes sin on the spiritual
plane, and sickness on the physical.

We become conscious of disorder only
when it causes us pain; hence we are apt
to confound it with pain, which is a serious
mistake.   Pain is man's perception of his
lack of conformity to God's idea of him.

It is a sign of life, — a sign that the Divine idea is deeply implanted in man. We feel pain spiritually just in proportion as the ideal is revealed to us, and we become aware how far we are from perfectly expressing it. This perception comes to us slowly on the spiritual plane, because the spiritual ideal is not distinct to the mass of mankind and thoroughly accepted by them. On the physical plane, however, the ideal is clearer. The reason it hurts a man to cut his finger is that his finger is meant to be whole. The perfect ideal of our bodies is so inborn in us, so much a part of our life, that we are not conscious of it until it is impaired in some way. It is a common saying that only the sick know how to appreciate health.

Pain is a sign of life, but also a sign that life is not yet perfect. We are born with this imperfection; and because the process of driving it out by turning to God for more perfect development involves an

acceptance of pain, in other words a sacrifice, we, from a mistaken fear of pain, turn
away from God and thereby store up more
and more pain for ourselves in the greater
wrench with which we must turn back to
Him by and by. Thus, pain even unto
death has become necessary for man in
order to free him from his captivity to
material things, and prove to him that the
only reality is in God. Pain is the measure
of man's divergence from his true life, but
it is also the pledge of his return to it.
Because God and our perfection in Him
is the only reality, man is bound — tied
by cords which he may strain but cannot
break — to return and conform himself to
God at last. Man by his struggles makes
pain a devil to hold him captive through
fear, when it should be an angel to lead
him to God through faith.

If pain is not an essential part of sin and
sickness, what are these when considered
in themselves? Merely disorder, — imper-

fect expression; bitter realities to us so long as we accept them and let our fear of pain hinder our turning from them to God, but mere mal-adjustments, soon to be remedied, if we face resolutely our ideal, and accept with joy the healing pain that comes with the self-revelation involved therein. The special point made by the mental healers is, that this truth applies in physical as well as in spiritual relations, because all life is really one. In other words, if man can be led to turn his whole being towards God, he will be freed from sickness as well as from sin; because all material things, including every atom of man's body, will then fall into harmony and order, becoming, as they were meant to be, truly expressive of God's thought. If, on the other hand, man is not wholly turned towards God; if, though believing in the reality of the spiritual life, he still doubts its power over the body, — still doubts that spiritual life includes all other life, — then disease, the physical disorder that exists in us all because we are not yet purely expressive of God's thought, has for him a reality which holds him in thrall until he is led to turn away from it, and by that turning destroy its existence for himself and for others.

A most important point is the question of reality as related to man. The Real is the royal, the ruling power. It is life, it is God; all else is negation and death. In so far as man accepts God and becomes like God, disorder ceases to rule, — that is, to have a reality for him. Sin and sickness may become unreal to man if he chooses to make them so. Man stands between two possible realities, — spirit and matter.[1] Either may become positive, or ruling, to him according as he believes in it, and by his belief becomes himself the complement

[1] We say "matter," but we really mean that spirit of negation and despair which is the only voice that speaks to us through matter when we look at it apart from God.

of it. Whichever he thus makes positive and real to himself causes the other to become negative and have but an inverted existence for him. Man's freedom would seem to make it a matter of indifference which he should choose; but in truth the whole force of creation is set to make him choose wisely and recognize spiritual things. His only chance for health and happiness, and for solving the problems of existence, lies in his lending faith to, and thereby making real to himself, the spiritual life centring in God. Thus, man's "free agency," in its right — and in the end only possible — outworking, is seen to be identical with God's "sovereignty." In proportion as man resolutely sets his being in the direction of God, the natural life and all material things have but a negative and inverted existence for him; but — and this is the strangest part of all — the natural life and all material things when standing in this negative and inverted relation to man are found to express a harmony, beauty, and use that they had only hinted at before. They become pure expressions of God's thought, and therefore full of all that is beautiful and wholesome. Being no longer confounded with the thought they were made to express, they become immaterial in both senses of the word; that is, they become un-material, transparent to the Divine idea, and immaterial in the sense of unimportant, because, having done their work and delivered their message, they can be safely changed and transmuted, as we scatter the type with which a sentence has been printed, in order to use it again to print a different one. It is along this line of thought that the believers in the Mind Cure foresee for man an ultimate spiritual control over all the forces of Nature. We have only the smallest beginning of it as yet; but that we have any at all is proof of the rest. Full control cannot come to man until he understands and accepts perfectly God's idea as expressed in every material atom, — in other words, until his will becomes completely identified with God's will; because not until then can he be sure of making no changes except such as are perfectly in accord with that law or being of God which is Life.

As soon as man is capable of perceiving order and harmony (that is, as soon as he rises above the brutes), he sees traces of them in material things, and he also sees infractions of them there resulting from the interaction of forces not yet wholly harmonized. It is natural for him to believe that the order, as well as the disorder, inhere in material things as such. The great lesson for him to-day is that *he* is the key of the situation; that in him it lies to make more and more disorder by so believing in material things that they become real, or ruling, to him, or to bring order, harmony, and joy to the whole world of Nature by making his life so tributary to God that through him all Nature becomes obedient and finds a voice to speak the word enshrined in it from the beginning, namely, Eternal Life. On man lies the responsibility; to him is given the honor of thus turning the creation right side out; of giving to each form on earth its right explanation, and thereby revealing that form to itself.

A deeper perception of the nature of life produces a keener sense of the responsibility and prerogative of man; and conversely, in proportion as man shoulders his responsibility and uses his prerogative, the nature of life is unfolded to him. Mental Healing has made an advance in both these directions. It has dared assume man's highest prerogative, — that of bringing life to men from God, and has gained a profound sense of what life really is.

Life may be broadly defined as mutual recognition. Life absolute exists only in

God, who is the source of all real life.
Man never truly lives till he recognizes
God.   God does not wait for man's recognition in order to live, because with
Him this long delay which we call time
does not exist.   The end and the beginning — Alpha and Omega — are one in
mutual recognition in Him.   Our perfection already exists in Him, and answers to
His thought and love.   The whole healing
virtue of the Mind Cure lies in its absolute faith in this great truth, — that man's
perfection is already complete in God.

Life is mutual recognition.   Half-life,
or existence, results from cognition by a
higher type.   The vegetable world exists
by virtue of cognition by the animal; animals depend for cognition on man, and
are in a degree capable of re-cognizing
him and thereby attaining a more complete life than is possible for the plant.
This process, whereby each grade of life
sustains the grades below itself, goes on

unconsciously to us, because our belief in
material forms is so inborn that our life
flows out to them without our being aware
of it.   It is not until we are startled into
questioning our relation to them, that we
begin to withdraw our confidence in their
apparent reality, which thereby receives
its first death-blow.   We are in no way
to blame for the support that goes out
from us towards material things, nor do
we in any way suffer from it so long as
it is unconscious.   It is only when our
confidence in them has been shaken by
intimations of our higher life, of the true
reality, that we become self-conscious, —
that is, aware of our lack of adjustment
to God the Real.   Then the process of
detachment from material things must go
on more and more, and we involve ourselves in much trouble and confusion if
we continue to allow any form or idea
below ourselves to rule us.   Our whole
responsibility lies in recognizing God as

the real, the only ruling, positive force
of the universe. Man cannot make both
God and material things positive to himself at the same time; therefore, if he
makes God positive to himself, he turns
to material things as their master. Himself the positive pole to them, he forces
them into that negative attitude in which
their only true and indestructible reality
consists; because then alone do they express the divine order, life being passed
on to them through man from God, in
due sequence. Man thus stands as an in-
telligent pivot upon whom, and by whose
aid, the whole creation is to turn to the
light. He has power to communicate life
to all lower forms just in proportion as
he receives life from God. If he looks at
a temptation with fear that he shall yield
to it, whether that temptation take the
form of a spiritual or a physical disorder;
if he doubts God's power in him to tri-
umph over it, then the temptation becomes

the positive or ruling pole to him, and has
an existence in him which quickly develops into sin on the spiritual plane or into
sickness on the physical.   If, on the other
hand, he refuses to recognize the temptation and turns from it to God, he draws
from Him who is forever the Great Positive, the great I AM, supplies of real life,
which passing through man drive out all
disorder by bringing both soul and body
to their right attitude at the negative pole.
This service one man can in a measure
do for another.   We can make ourselves
mediums of the Divine life in each other's
behalf.   We can receive so much of it
through our love for and belief in them,
as we see them in God, that we become
positive to them, and so pass along to
them the current of life in such manner
as to drive out their diseases and break
into their prison cells of discouragement
and despair.

It is on the perception of this power that

all Mental Healing is founded. Because all life is one, every human being can, according to his faith and knowledge, see for another the ideal of that other, quarrying it as it were out of the unseen, and bringing it so close to the needy one that it conforms his feebleness to itself. We all do this unconsciously for our friends when we have faith in their best possibility. Mental Healing goes one step farther, and by grasping the reality of God so intensely that all things are as nothing in comparison, it brings the Divine life so close to human suffering as to reach the inmost depths of the physical being and drive out disease.

There is a dark side to all this which one would willingly ignore, but which demands a few words. A measure of control over natural forces and over feeble human wills is sometimes attained by men of great nervous energy, whose belief in themselves is so positive as to force other

elements into a negative attitude. Such
persons would be most effective for good
if they recognized the source of their
power as the Infinite Spirit of love and
wisdom, for then they could will only such
changes in others as tend to health and
blessedness. Failing in this recognition,
the work of human wills is not only dis-
orderly, but sometimes even malicious,
and may do much temporary mischief.
But it is not after all greatly to be feared,
because it is self-limited. It is mere re-
flex action stimulated by the forms and
influences of the external world, and, like
all idolatry, all imputing to the creature
the functions of the Creator, all making
real anything less than God, it is sure to
be overthrown and brought to nought, for
the very simple reason that the unconse-
crated human will soon becomes so out of
relation to the only source of real life
that its supply is cut off and its power
ceases.

THE PRACTICE OF MENTAL HEALING.

THE PRACTICE OF MENTAL HEALING.

HERE we come to facts and to methods. There is one class of facts which is ignored by those who have written about Mental Healing, but which is most significant. It is the almost universal testimony of those who have been treated, that they have received great benefit in moral and spiritual directions, manifesting itself in greater harmony of character and improved intellectual soundness and balance. Numerous persons have attended lectures on Mental Healing whose physical condition did not need improving, but who were interested in the truth itself. These have

found it a great inspiration and help; and
it is worth while to make note of their experience as an offset to the stories, not
infrequently told, of the failures and mal-
practice of those who undertake to cure
by the new methods. Failures there certainly are, and ill-judged applications of
the truth, doubtless; but let us remember
that the science is in its infancy, and has
yet much wisdom to learn. We may hope
that it will never have to give account for
worse misdeeds than already disfigure the
annals of medicine.

We have said that the Mind Cure and
the Faith Cure are two different phases of
the same school. The Mind Cure is by no
means without the element of faith; but
it hopes, by making no demand for faith
at the outset, to reach many who might
otherwise be repelled by such a demand.
Those who seek its aid only because they
have exhausted all other means of help, or
those who come merely at the solicitation

of friends, are successfully healed, as well as those whose spiritual development has already fitted them to receive the doctrines. A mental attitude of resolute opposition or contempt is a serious barrier to any good work; but if the attitude is merely negative, the simple fact that a person submits himself to an influence which uses no material means, argues sufficient faith on his part to render it possible for the healer to make a beginning. Later, when successive treatments have caused the seed of right life which is in every human being to germinate and put forth shoots, instruction is given, either individually or in classes, and the patient is led, according to his capacity, to recognize the Divine Spirit that is working in him, and to trust it and appeal to it independently of the efforts of the healer. The great point made by the Mind, as distinguished from the Faith Cure, is that this awakening of the patient's personal faith in unseen

things is not attempted till it has been
proved to him, by his own experience,
that beneficent physical changes can be
wrought in him without visible or material
means. He is then prepared for faith; not
prepared to receive the old theological dog-
mas, perhaps, but prepared to believe, and
put his trust in, an unseen benevolent
power. When once this growth of soul is
started, the man's allegiance is transferred
from the material to the spiritual pole of
life. This is the "change of heart," or
"new birth," which all true religion seeks
to bring about, and which, if our spiritual
senses were acute enough to discern it,
would appear as real and as startling as
if the person experiencing it were being
turned the other side out. The change
does show itself, even to our bodily eyes,
in the gracious smile and outreaching expression which replace the troubled and
gloomy looks that went before. Artists
have recognized the contrast from the days

of Da Vinci[1] to the present time, when Vedder paints for us the hesitation of the Soul between Doubt and Faith. In this picture the head of Faith is a novel conception, but quite in accord with the truth we are trying to state. Faith has usually been represented with upraised eyes, as though spiritual realities could only be discerned by turning away from the life that now is. Vedder's Faith is of a more robust type. It looks serenely *out* instead of up; daring to face all earthly pain and confusion because of its utter reliance on the Divine power which will, in the end, reduce all things to order.

Now, if the change from doubt to faith, which is the great thing to be desired for us all, can be brought about by Mental

---

[1] In the Sciarra Palace at Rome is a picture designed by Da Vinci, but painted by Luini. It bears the title "Vanity and Modesty," but is in fact a profound study of two contrasted types, — the life that centres wholly around self, and the life that reaches out in care and thought for others.

Healing, what are the methods whereby it is accomplished? In what do the so-called " treatments " consist?

It may boldly be asserted that the treatments are prayer, and prayer in its most prevailing form. Prayer may be best defined as the effort of the human will to place itself in perfect accord with the Divine will. To achieve this we may pour out our burdened hearts in specific petitions and close them with the name of Christ (which embodies for us the supreme sacrifice of the human will to the Divine), thus signifying that if we have not prayed aright we trust that God will be wiser than our prayers. This is prayer as most of us know it. An increased consciousness of God in us and in all things will, however, tend to simplify our prayers. When we realize God as perfect wisdom and perfect love, we shall see that He needs neither instruction nor appeal; that on His part all is done even before we ask it. Therefore prayer chiefly concerns ourselves, and others like us in whom ignorance, doubt, and self-will hinder the workings of that perfect love and perfect wisdom to which we appeal. Here prayer has an immense field, in bringing us, and our short-sighted plans and rebellious wishes, into harmony with our highest and best selves, — that is, God's idea of us. This is exactly what the treatments of mental healers accomplish. The person who gives the treatment sets his whole soul to the work, and sees with absolute conviction the ideal perfection of the unconscious individual before him; sees it for the patient, — thus transferring his whole spiritual energy to the case of another, to serve that other's need in the true spirit of love. Treatments like this may be given by any one as soon as he has grasped the fundamental truth that God's will is perfect for each and all. If he doubts this, and thinks that the special case before him is an

exception, and that so much error and sickness as the patient exhibits must argue a
very limited possibility for that patient,
the treatment will fall flat and powerless.
It is only the sublime faith that is almost
sight, a faith that dares take its stand in
the very heart of God, that can avail.

This central truth is in a way the simplest truth, because faith is always a short
cut compared with knowledge. Treatments given in this way are often very
effective, because if the centre is moved
the circumference is bound to follow. This
explains the success of many beginners.
Knowledge, however, is needed to compact
and define the steps up which faith hastens
with rapid flight. Those who are distinguished in Mental Healing learn by long
practice, and by trusting their spiritual
perceptions, to see how cause and effect
are related one to the other, and how the
special disease of the person under treatment is caused by some special spiritual

incompleteness. They can therefore ad-
dress their treatment to the particular qual-
ity of soul which needs to be developed,
and thus be more effective than a person
who treats with less understanding.

All this seems perhaps somewhat remote from the immediate question of
physical health, the search for which has
been the means of drawing so many to
what ere long they discovered to be a
higher spiritual life. But the question remains, "Did they find the physical health
they sought?" In many cases they have
found it, speedily and to a degree almost miraculous; in other cases the im-
provement has been slower, and some
have gone away disappointed. These
varying results are due to the varying capacity of individuals to be affected from
the spiritual side, to the variety of outside influences to which the patient is sub-
jected, and to the varying nature and cause
of the diseases treated. All persons can be

affected by Mental Healing if they yield
themselves to it fully and for a sufficient
length of time; but those who have least
faith, or openness to spiritual things, are
the most difficult to reach, and these
are precisely the ones whose patience gives
out soonest, and who abandon the treatment in disgust, saying, "I told you so!"
Then, even those who are themselves willing to believe are often held back and
seriously hindered by the atmosphere of
doubt and ridicule which they meet at
home. Possibly they are also continuing
some other form of treatment all the time
that they are receiving Mental Healing,
with the notion that safety lies in having
two strings to one's bow. This is a very
serious hindrance, and is forbidden for the
same reason that drugs are forbidden;
namely, that dependence on them or any
other material means leads the patient to
look in the wrong direction, and so defeats
the tremendous effort which is being made

by the healer to lift the unconscious soul past the dead point and start all its energies in the direction of life and health.

In regard to the varying nature of disease, it is obvious that if the Mind Cure is a genuine spiritual agent, it will reach most easily the nervous system, which is the most susceptible part of our organization. It is the glory of Mental Healing that it does reach and heal those nervous maladies which have increased in number so alarmingly of late years, and which so often baffle a physician's skill. Even its opponents are forced to admit this. Functional disease is treated with conspicuous success. How, then, about organic disease? It is harder to see how this can be cured; but according to our premises the centre will move the circumference: therefore if the currents of life can be set moving in the right direction, every particle of the human frame is bound in time to be affected by that rightness. If our philosophy be true,

we must remember that diseased matter
has in itself no power of opposition; that
a cancer, for instance, has no power to live
and grow in us except as by our recognition we make it positive to ourselves, thereby imputing to it the reality that belongs
only to God.

Will broken bones set themselves at the
bidding of mental healers? They do not
claim this. They set no limit to the power
of the Spirit they invoke, because they
know that it is infinite; but they also
know that spirit can be brought to bear
upon matter only in proportion to man's
belief in spirit, and that is at present very
small. What Mental Healing can and does
do is to bring life to men from God. All
disorder that can be driven out of the
human system by a full current from the
true Source of being, will in time disappear
under the influence of Mental Healing, and
will disappear at a much faster rate when
the world's atmosphere is more largely

made up of belief in unseen things than it is at present. What we should now consider a miracle in the way of conforming an undeveloped physical frame to its ideal perfection will probably then be a common occurrence. Restoration, however, whether it be the reconstruction of lost limbs or the complete rescue of man's body from its apparent defeat by death, will require an outpouring of life such as can only become possible when the consciousness of mankind shall rest so habitually in the spiritual realm that all physical expression — that is, the body or any part of it — will be a matter of indifference, to be assumed or laid aside at will. When that time comes, we shall not fear being killed or maimed, because it will be impossible to do it. The real life, which we shall then recognize in our every fibre, cannot be touched by any weapon of mortal warfare.

But it is unwise to speak too much in this spirit of prophecy, lest it discourage

the timid faith of many who are quite willing to believe in small things; and that this
is but the day of small things we are ready
to admit.   It is one of the chief dangers of
those who practise Mental Healing, that in
the atmosphere of that wonderful realm in
which many of their hours are spent, they
lose the sense of time and realize future
things so vividly as to dream them actually
present.   For this cause they are apt to
make specific promises of cure and set
times for their fulfilment.   Then, if from
obstacles that they had not reckoned on,
that fulfilment is delayed, the effect on the
patient's mind is discouraging.

As to the cause of disease.   Broadly
speaking, disease is caused by sin or wrong-
ness of life; in other words, by inhar-
monious spiritual conditions.   What, then,
explains the diseases of good persons, or
of children, idiots, and others who are not
responsible?   The first answer to this is
the mighty truth that no one of us liveth

or dieth to himself. This solidarity of the race is forced upon our consciousness more and more every day. Our thoughts, our beliefs, our errors affect others often more than they affect ourselves; we suffer for the sins of our ancestors, and our own sins work woe for our children. It is easy to see how this comes to pass in the direct line of descent; but when the Mind Cure makes the statement that the general belief in a disease — scarlet fever, for instance — is sufficient to produce that disease in a baby, or sufficient to bring some serious malady, not hereditary, to a person leading a faithful and upright life, the statement certainly calls for explanation.

Here we must go back to our philosophy. God is One. All real life is One, because life is God. Each human being is such in virtue of his ability to accept or refuse that Life. By accepting it he finds his true individuality, and discovers that by it he is linked to all the rest of mankind, and is responsible for and to them in a way that he never dreamed before. His life is so bound up with that of every other human creature, that when he believes in and accepts disease for himself he does it also for the race, and thus the common consciousness becomes the home of every recognized malady.

If, then, in acting for ourselves we act for all the rest of mankind, it only remains to explain how we create disease for ourselves. We do it by the human will when that will acts independently of the Divine will. Will may be defined as the force proceeding from belief, and has a distinct creative power. Man's will creates indirectly by the use of material means, as when he builds a house or ship; but he has a more direct power of creating which inheres in him because he is made in God's image. This is something that he has not yet begun to measure. The power of belief, and will proceeding from belief, to create and to destroy outside the realm of matter will some day be understood as man's highest attribute and deepest responsibility. At present the full knowledge of it is withheld lest he should use his power impiously. So long as man's will works with God's will he creates good and heavenly things which endure. If he builds a house on scientific principles, it stands, and its drains do not breed disease; or, on a higher plane, the man who wills only love and truth to his neighbor, rears for himself lasting monuments in the shape of noble institutions and quickened lives. But if he works only with self-will, looking away from God, he creates the evil things of which hell is made. The falsely constructed railway bridge crushes in its pit of death a thousand happy lives because it was not built according to law; so on the spiritual plane man's will, man's belief, if it looks away from God, actually creates disease.

How can man will to create disease if he does not wish to create it? He does not will to create the disease, but he wills or has willed, perhaps many generations back, those evil deeds which produce disease. The seed thus sown, fostered by belief and fear, in time attains a spurious entity, terribly real in appearance, but which nevertheless depends wholly for its life upon the recognition and belief of man.

A few words about belief may help us here. Belief may be defined as acceptance. Acceptance by a human spirit of any suggestion confirms and gives reality to that suggestion which forthwith develops and manifests itself in acts as if it had in itself a propagating power. We know that the suggestion would have had no such power if it had fallen on deaf ears so that it could not be accepted or believed in. In the realm of ethics this is the simplest of truths; why may it not also be true in physical conditions? A man is threatened with consumption, we will say; the idea of consumption, which had never been in his mind before, now confronts him at every turn, because physical symptoms constantly remind him of it. Is it too much to say that his acceptance of or belief in this idea has an actual power to confirm and develop the idea, and consequently the disease also? If our premises are true, and spirit rather than matter is the real causing force, there can be but one answer to this. For those who do not accept our premises, the whole argument falls to the ground. But it remains for such persons to explain how physical changes can be brought about by the Mind Cure treatments, which are purely spiritual; and that such changes are brought about there is abundant evidence, of which any one may satisfy himself.

In addition to the belief of the sick person about his own disease, there is, as we have said, a general human acceptance of

disease in the abstract, as a sort of roaring
lion seeking whom he may devour, which
is a solid support and encouragement to it.
Then the belief of all the invalid's friends
about his disease helps greatly to give it
reality, especially if the disease can be
called hereditary in his family, so that the
acceptance of past generations rolls thun-
dering into his heart with a voice of fate-
ful prophecy.

The disease once accepted, fear comes
in as a most powerful agent in developing it.

What is fear? Nothing but the absence
of that absolute and enfolding peace which
is ours when we live wholly with the Divine
life and in conformity to its laws. Fear
may be, like most things, an angel or a
devil to us according as we use it from the
spiritual or the material pole of life. It
may be a warning note; it may also be the
hot-bed of all evil growths. Just as pure
desire, the soul's passion for God and

righteousness, and for all things that minister to that righteousness, has for its guarantee and seal that peace of which we have just spoken, so evil desire, the lust for things against the conscience, has for its concomitant and undivorcible shadow fear, which ever fosters lust and drives it forward in its hideous course, closing up the way behind and barring the pathway of return. Thus fear has an actual fostering power, and develops all evil growths just as surely as peace, once tasted as the result of pure living, produces a deathless thirst for higher spiritual attainments, ever approved by deeper peace.

Now, if this be true of fear in ethical relations, may we not extend the statement to the physical realm, as we did the statement about belief? A disease once started is to the body what a sin is to the soul. It is an inharmony, a wrong action, breaking up the peace which we feel when all is well, and producing in its stead fear, which, if indulged, has an undreamed-of power to increase and develop the very thing it seems to dread. Thus, wrong belief and fear are powerful enough in the under world to give disease all the entity it has, — the spurious entity of a devil, — so that it actually has a sinister power to fasten itself on an unconscious person and grow in him to great stature, unless checked by an influx of the true life. Let us understand fear, and use it aright. If we learn to think of it only as we ought to think, — namely, as a note of warning, — then it is transformed into one of God's angels, who are charged to keep us in all our ways. When we fear that a disease has attacked us, instead of fearing the disease itself, which is but to recognize it and develop it with tenfold power, let us so far as possible turn our thoughts away from the physical manifestation called disease, while we set our whole energy to round out the incompleteness, to root out the wrong feeling, thought, or habit, of which the disease is but the outward sign. Then fear becomes an angel of help, and with God on our side we conquer and are healed. And we conquer not only for ourselves, but for our children, for our race; because every one who casts out and conquers fear, so that it has no existence for him except as a warning of moral or spiritual danger, is henceforth freed from disease, and his free and healthful life exerts a powerful influence in destroying disease in his family and in those about him.

It may be objected, in this connection, that there are many recorded instances in which a bedridden invalid has recovered the use of his limbs through fear of some immediate catastrophe, — the house catching fire, for example, — and that therefore fear is curative. We must here discriminate between fear and fright. We have said that fear is curative when rightly used. If fear drives a man out of himself towards

God, — that is, if it leads him to forsake the wrong moral and physical conditions which have induced it, — then it becomes curative in the highest sense. The danger is, however, that fear, instead of producing this wholesome reaction, will only benumb its victim, and draw him more and more under the spell of some threatened evil. The superiority of fright over fear as a curative agent lies in its suddenness, which drives the man out of himself before he has time to fall under the paralyzing spell of danger; and whatever drives a man out of himself, really drives him in the direction of God, though it may be long ere he discovers this and manifests it by a more faithful life. A good scare is often all that is needed to bring about an absolute letting go of the human will; and this letting go may start a man's life out of its physical prison and restore to him the use of his limbs. When he recovers from his *fright* and finds that he has once used his limbs successfully, he is freed thenceforth from the paralyzing *fear* of not being able to move them, which had been his trouble all along.

Until we can see the spiritual being of man as plainly as we now see his material form, we cannot tell precisely how a given disease was produced in a given case; but of one thing we may be sure, — it has all come about according to inevitable law.

Material processes of various degrees of complication are required to effect various material results. It is the same with spiritual processes, which must be more elaborate and protracted to heal some maladies than others; and this accounts for the differing lengths of time and degrees of success in the treatments of Mental Healing. Not until its practitioners can see and measure all the influences involved, can they work with absolute certainty and precision; but that will come in time, and meanwhile they have the key of the situation, and can open many a hitherto locked door.   Some cases yield very quickly. Sometimes in a well-balanced and healthy physique the whole trouble, rheumatism, dyspepsia, or whatever it may be, arises from a suppressed grief, an unforgiving spirit, a fault-finding temper, or some such immediate cause.   If these are removed, the sickness disappears at once.   In other cases, where the cause is more remote, the cure comes more slowly; but in all cases the method of cure is the same.   The healer sets his whole being at work to form a mental image of the patient *as that patient ought to be,* — free from sin, free from disease, in a state of complete development and harmony.   He holds this image with great tenacity for a certain length of time, usually about fifteen minutes, and then the treatment is at an end.   It may seem incredible, but this mental image has a vital power to conform the suffering, imperfect body of the patient to itself; and why? Only because it is really God's thought of the man, perceived by the faith of the healer, who thus performs an office of atonement, by bringing God's perfect thought and man's imperfect expression of it — namely, his sickly body — together. It is a well-attested fact that right vital action, both physical and spiritual, does develop in consequence of these Mind Cure treatments.

Miss Frances Power Cobbe, in a recent article in the " Contemporary Review," entitled, " Faith healing and Fear killing," says that the first question to be answered, in any inquiry into the subject, is, whether the healing virtue affects directly the body of the patient, or whether it only affects the patient's mind, which in its turn affects the patient's body. The true answer to this question is, that it affects both, for the two are, according to the Mind Cure, really one. The body is only the expression in material terms of the informing mind, or spirit. The effect of Mental Healing is first felt by the patient on the spiritual or on the physical side of his being, according as his consciousness habitually rests in one or the other. Some persons are first aware of an increased spiritual vitality, and the physical symptoms are the last to yield. With others the physical derangement may be set right first, causing the vital currents to flow outward with such a fresh sense of freedom that they raise the soul to new life and hope.[1]

[1] There is one point respecting Mental Healing which is theologically of much interest. While it aims at spiritual regeneration (and at physical regeneration only through the spiritual), it works towards this end without exciting the opposition of the patient. Religion, with the same end in view, by presenting God as external to the individual, rouses man's sense of all in which he differs from the Divine idea. This sense, known in religious parlance as "conviction of sin," produces a state of conflict or rebellion against God until man, by surrendering his will to the Divine will, finds peace. Mental Healing, on the other hand, assuming that God is in every individual, addresses itself silently to the Divine idea in each of its patients, and

" Absent Treatments " are a distinguishing feature of Mental Healing. Acting on the conviction that all real life is one in God, and therefore independent of the conditions of space, the healers frequently treat persons who are separated from them by thousands of miles. Results justify their faith. Convincing testimony may be had of the power of such treatments, which are given sometimes with, and sometimes without, the knowledge of the patient.

by developing that idea *from within* it fills them with an impulse towards the best, and opens their eyes to their highest possibility, without rousing opposition by presenting that idea as external to themselves. The whole difference between the Mind Cure position and the old-fashioned theological position may be summed up by saying that the former assumes God to be in every man the rightful sovereign, and selfhood an imprisoning wall built of human error which debars the sovereign from his proper sway ; while the latter assumes selfhood to be all there is of man, from centre to circumference, and by such assumption endows the unregenerate man with a reality, a power of opposition, which in fact does not exist ; though the power seems real enough, and will continue to seem so, until, by withdrawing our belief from it, we destroy its reality.

We have said that life is mutual recognition; or, expressing the same thought in a less ideal form, life is the interaction of two opposing currents. This may help us to understand the subtle distinction between the Mind Cure and the Faith Cure. Two elements must enter into the regeneration of a human being in order to fill him with a higher life. One is the ideal of that being, God's perfect thought of him, towards which, through many vicissitudes, he is tending; the other is the recognition and acceptance of that ideal by the human being himself. One is the Divine, — the positive current reaching down to the human; the other is the negative, recipient, human current reaching up to the Divine. The Mind Cure addresses its work first to the former element, the Faith Cure to the latter; and as each current involves the other, neither method is quite independent of the other.

The Mind Cure uses all its power to lay

hold of and bring to bear in unseen ways the Divine ideal of the patient, trusting to the spiritual force of that ideal to conform the patient, soul and body, to itself. Later it imparts wisdom by instruction, and assures its patients that their cure will not be lasting except as they voluntarily open their souls to make the Divine will and goodness their own. If a man could transgress all the laws of health, and then escape the consequences merely by taking fifteen minutes' treatment, he would not grow to be a better man; and we may accept it as the certainty of certainties that the perfecting of every human soul is the real and final cause of the whole mechanism called matter.

The Faith Cure, on the other hand, uses all its power to start the human, recipient life-current out of its mortal prison, so that meeting the ever-present Divine current it enables that Divine current to enter the sufferer and fill him with new life.

To achieve this, it is not at first necessary that the patient should form an intel-
ligent conception of the ideal; and in fact
the Faith Cure helps chiefly those whose
hearts are more easily moved than their
heads.   But it succeeds because things are
so linked together in the good providence
of God that anything which raises a man
out of himself brings him a little nearer
to his ideal perfection.   Veneration for an
inanimate relic or for some professed miracle-worker may achieve this, but there is
always an attendant risk.   If the patient
grows in intelligence, he soon sees beyond
the object or person by whom his faith
was first aroused, and before he can transfer his allegiance and veneration to some
higher and more worthy object there is
danger of his letting go and losing his
faith altogether.   Safety lies in offering at
once to soul and body no less a reality
than God Himself.

MENTAL HEALING AS RELATED TO OTHER TRUTH.

MENTAL HEALING AS RELATED TO OTHER TRUTH.

THREE statements made by the teachers of Mental Healing lay its doctrines open to the charge of absurdity. These are — 1. That disease is not a reality; 2. That all material remedies are useless if not mischievous; 3. That sickness and death are not the will of God.

Before attempting to answer these charges separately, we may say in general that the extreme position taken by the doctrine of Mental Healing is no more extreme than that taken by Religion, Science, or any other great working hypothesis. When we look at things simply as philosophers, we see more truths than are at once available for practical use. A man may have his hands too full of weapons to go to war. When we are in the line of achievement we must select some weapons and discard others. Science, seeking facts and working by analysis, feels that she must stop her ears to the voice of the Spirit, lest in the self-forgetfulness of listening she should overlook a single fact or blunder in a single process. On the other hand, Religion often slights or ignores obvious facts, and in her determination to compass worthy ends is in danger of leaving some most essential element out of her problem. Science and Religion are like two children set in a room to pick up and re-string a thousand scattered pearls which form a girdle. Science, kneeling to the pearls, seeks them in every corner with tireless persistence, and almost forgets the golden thread which alone can hold them together after they are found, so that chaos and dispersion cannot come again. Her sister stands aloof grasping the two ends of the golden thread, and is in such haste to knot these together in a perfect girdle again, that she makes light of the importance of each separate individual pearl, and is restless and vexed when Science tells her that the girdle cannot be perfect so long as one pin-point of a pearl is left out.

Now, it is evident that each of these handmaidens of the Lord is shutting her eyes to one class of facts, and that neither will revolutionize the world without the other's help. The philosophy of which Mental Healing is the practical expression, seems at first, when crudely stated, to be at issue with both, but may end by reconciling the two. When it says that disease is unreal, man's body a shadow, and all material remedies useless, Science, especially medical science which is occupied with the needs of the body, feels that if this be true her whole occupation and charter are taken away. When we are told that sickness and death are not God's will, Religion, which has won her highest triumphs by reconciling men to such afflictions on the ground that they are God's will, feels the very foundations trembling beneath her feet.

Thus the new philosophy makes extreme statements in two opposite directions; but does it not stretch forth a hand of sympathy in two opposite directions also? Does not the assertion of the unreality of all material things lie at the very heart of a religion whose Founder said, "Whosoever he be of you that forsaketh not all that he hath, he cannot be my disciple"? On the other hand, shall not Science, whose watchword is evolution by the inevitable sequence of natural law, welcome as an ally the voice which says that sickness and death are not the will of God? This means, in scientific parlance, that evolution must go on until there is no more work for it to do; that the seal of Divine approval cannot be finally set — in other words, the process of evolution cannot cease — until a creature is produced so perfectly fitted to all surrounding conditions that he stands triumphant over sickness and death. This will undoubtedly be brought about by the " survival of the fittest; " but we begin to see that because man's spiritual environment is more controlling than his physical one, earth's great Survivor must be he who is fittest physically *because he is fittest spiritually.* He alone can never be overthrown. He is the Christ.

We will now take up the three objections in detail, beginning with the statement that disease is not a reality. The abstract ground for saying this was explained in an earlier chapter. It remains to consider the practical outworking of the position. A careful statement of the truth would be that disease has no reality, or power to rule, and maintains itself in man in opposition to the will or life of God, except as man by his belief in and fear of disease endows it with such power. The great desideratum is to turn the patient towards belief in life and away from belief in death. By such turning he withdraws the support of his vitality from the disease, which thenceforth is unreal and cannot rule him. Until he does this, the disease is real to him; but no statement is too strong which can, by breaking up his belief in its reality, encourage him to face towards the Source of all true life, and thereby prove or *make true* that which before was only a matter of faith; namely, the unreality of the disease. It is to be observed that this is no passive ignoring of the malady, but an active and vigorous turning away from it in full faith that the very act of turning strikes a blow at its vitals.

To ignore a disease is not to cure it.

A superficial understanding of the statement that disease is not a reality, might lead a person to think that in case a serious malady threatens us, all we have to do is to ignore it resolutely and go on living just as we did before, in unwholesome conditions perhaps, or under some strain of overwork. Such a course would be folly. Its effect would be to encourage the disease by opposition; for while the patient flattered himself that he was ignoring his complaint, he would really be opposing his strength to it day by day in a losing battle, and thereby developing the disease and making it real. If with a better understanding he says bravely to himself, "This disease has no reality which can for an instant compare with the reality of God, therefore I will turn my life wholly to Him, make myself pliant in each detail and circumstance to His will, and seek from Him in all right ways those currents of life which shall drive out everything in me to

which disease can cling, " then, though the
process may be long, the cure is already
begun.

Secondly, the teachers of Mental Healing say that material remedies are useless
if not mischievous, and demand that those
who seek their treatment shall abandon the
use of medicine. This sounds like an un-
reasonable position until we realize how
great a risk a sick person runs of having
his life completely introverted by the average medical treatment. The doctor says
to one threatened with disease, " You must
give up your plan of life and devote your-
self to your health. You must seek exactly the right climate, travelling from
place to place in pursuit of it if necessary.
You must take this mixture to relieve
one symptom, and that mixture to relieve
another," and so on, till the man's whole
attention is turned away from his study,
business, or whatever was drawing him
in a healthy manner out of himself, and is

turned in upon his own body and his own sensations. The effect of this cannot but be bad, and the more remedies are multiplied the worse it becomes. Unquestionably change of climate is often beneficial, and remedies have their use, but the one thing absolutely indispensable is to keep the patient's life flowing outward in a strong current, — for on such right direction of his vital forces the whole question of recovery hangs. This is the *sine qua non*, it is life itself; and every material remedy, every change in outward circumstance, should wait humbly at the gate until its assistance is summoned by this Divine force. Many of our best physicians realize this truth, and are working to-day in the spirit of the Mind Cure without being aware of it.

No doubt drugs produce powerful and, where rightly applied, beneficent effects; but these touch the circumference rather than the centre of life in man. The new practice, in its effort to move men from the

centre, forbids the use of all material means
of cure, and takes thereby a position, which
if logically extended, would forbid also the
use of food. An extreme statement seems
to be the necessary weapon of the reformer.
When Mental Healing shall have established its point that man must be moved
first and chiefly from the spiritual side
even in physical matters, we shall find
that the Divine Spirit, instead of dispens-
ing with material means, is our one un-
erring guide to the wise use of such
means; teaching man to master them instead of letting them master him, which
is the danger to-day.

Multiplication of remedies, like specialization of practice, is part of the mod-
ern tendency, which is in all directions
to analyze, to discriminate, to subdivide.
Persons occupied in this way think they
are adding greatly to the sum of human knowledge, and that by each hair-
splitting they are securing a new unit.

This is a mistake. Subdivision never makes more, but less. It makes more *things*, perhaps, but less life, — and life is what men need. Specialization and analysis are good; but if we carry them too far we get the parts so out of relation to the whole that they are cut off and have no life in themselves. The more we can conscientiously group things together, overlooking minor differences, the better we see them in that relation to the whole which alone gives life to the parts; for be it said, in every language and in every place where a voice can be heard, *no part, no thing has any life in and of itself.* Life is God, the centre, dominating the whole; to look for it elsewhere is the most fatal of mistakes, and the degrees of this mistake sum up all the sin and suffering on earth.

Thirdly, sickness and death are not God's will for man. This strikes harshly on the ear of one who is just able to bear a crippling infirmity or a great bereave-

ment by accepting it as the will of God.
Truly, it is the will of God on a certain
plane; but because the condition of life
is growth, we must never rest satisfied on
any one plane of existence. God's will is
always the highest thing we can conceive
of, and as by our faith in it we bring that
highest thing to pass, our vision opens
to new spheres of life; thus God's will,
the Ideal, moves on, drawing us ever to
higher ends. The fatal mistake made by
man's faithlessness is that of arresting God's
will at any point and declaring such and
such a thing to be final. Perfection alone
can be final, because perfection is God.
Christians will agree that sickness and
death are not God's final will; but they
are slow to realize how immediate is the
duty imposed on man of bringing this final
will to pass here and now. The material
depths which faith can reach and regenerate are exactly in proportion to the heights
it climbs; and a new plane of development,

a new possibility for man, is opening to us to-day, the outcome of which will be a human body so perfect in every atom and fibre as to be a worthy "temple of the Holy Ghost." But this cannot come so long as we sit down under suffering, accepting it as God's will. Not that we are to maintain towards it an attitude of rebellion; but rather that we are to see beyond it to the perfect life that God's will holds for us all, and in the strength of that vision to pass fearlessly through pain to joy.

The question of planes and stages of development is a very important one, because most of our bad reasoning comes from mixing up these planes. What seems an obvious truth on one plane may change its guise completely when we reach the next, and yet be fundamentally the same truth on both. A careful study of these planes will help us to understand both why persons of low moral development often have good health, and also why persons of lovely and spiritual character are frequently invalids,— questions which puzzle us if we accept literally the truth that body and spirit are one, and are ruled by the same laws.

A man who lives wholly on the material or lowest plane may have good health for a time, because he is as undisturbed in the currents of his being as the animals are. He does not yet feel the discrepancy between his actual life and his ideal possibility. But this cannot last; he is made in the image of God, and to that image he is linked by desire. In his ignorance he fancies that desire can be satisfied by appropriating its object; so he steals from others money, life, or virtue, and his thirst is still unquenched. Such a course is sure to breed physical as well as social derangement, till the man's career is checked. His body is detained in prison perhaps for some infraction of law, and much more surely his life is imprisoned in his body, because instead of flowing healthily outward in love to God and man, it has all along been drawing inward towards himself. Because life is essentially the interaction of two currents, this drawing in cannot go on beyond a certain point; and unless the man learns that the secret of desire is to give rather than to receive, — in other words, that he can receive only by giving, — he goes on wrapping himself up tighter and tighter, until his imprisoned life works serious physical disturbance and his health is wrecked. By his mistaken idea of the meaning of desire he has made pain necessary for himself.

When suffering has taught him to abandon his evil practices, he enters on the next plane of existence with impaired physical vigor, but with a new understanding of the meaning of life. This may be only negative; it may debar him from the old paths without giving him any appetite for the new; he may merely say to himself that wrong-doing does not pay, but even this is a gain.

The lesson that life must flow outward is now repeated in a different form. The man is no longer in danger of having his life introverted by gross sin, but by his struggle against the physical limitations which his own errors have imposed on him. He beats the prison bars for years perhaps, until he learns to accept suffering as God's will. Then peace comes, and he grows upwards, bearing his pain cheerfully, and looking forward to the day when death shall give him freedom. This is the plane on which most Christian lives are lived.

On the first or physical plane God's will for the man appeared to him under the guise of pain, that he might cease from sin and enter the moral plane. On the second or moral plane it appears still under the guise of pain, that he may detach himself from his body more and more, and rise to the spiritual plane. Now another plane opens on which man may rise so high above his body as to *identify himself with the will or life of God.* When he does this perfectly, all physical disturbance will be rectified by the power of that life in him, and his body will be regenerated as well as his soul. If persons of spiritual character have not hitherto had good health, it is simply because their faith has not reached high enough to bring down to them such fulness of life as shall inundate, cleanse, and break through all the physical as well as moral stagnant places in their being.

The way out of our troubles may be through pain; but *if we cease from making more pain for ourselves by our struggles,* and accept what remains as simply curative, we pass through it swiftly and cheerfully, and by each victory we diminish the need of it for ourselves and for others. The body need not in the end be sacrificed to

the spirit. So long as it imprisons the
spirit it must be crushed, blasted even, by
the fearful dynamics of affliction and disease; but when it is once in its proper
place, at the feet of the spirit, obedient in
every atom and fibre to the highest law,
then we shall see the dawning of a heavenly
day when healthy bodies and healthy
spirits shall be inseparable, and when our
young people, wisely instructed and care-
fully nurtured, shall blossom from one
stage of life's beauty to the next without
a struggle.

Is death to be conquered? In the end,
yes. Living in that faith, we see the veil
between the two worlds grow thinner and
more transparent. As we abide in and
recognize only those things which belong
to the life of God, our spiritual senses un-
fold, and we find ourselves in a vast realm
which is the eternal home of all that conforms to its laws, regardless of time, space,
or material circumstance. Not one true,

pure, or loving thought has ever been lost since the world began, or ever can be lost, because these are of God, the only Reality. Just so far as our beloved who have passed from sight have embodied these thoughts they are indestructible, and await our recognition in that kingdom of heaven which is so near to each one of us that we may enter it at any moment if we will, and live evermore to the music of its harmonies.

CONCLUSION.

CONCLUSION.

WE begin to see that the human will, or spirit, is the great channel through which the Divine Spirit is to regenerate and harmonize the world of Nature. That this may come to pass, man's will must become both consecrated and enlightened. Religion calls us to the first duty, Science to the second. They are equally necessary, and neither can dispense with the other's help even in its own domain. A religious man may devote his life to helping his fellows, but he cannot do this with success, in fact he cannot remain long enough in this world to do it at all, except as he understands external conditions.

On the other hand, spiritual truth, which alone can reconcile all the facts of life, becomes the property of man only as a result of the surrender or consecration of the human will.

We have said that life is the interaction of two currents, — the human will reaching up to the Divine, and the Divine will reaching down to the human; and that because the Divine will is the master force, the human will must make itself the passive or receptive pole in this interchange if life is to stand on its right basis. It is the same with the appropriation of truth. Man's energy can accumulate facts to an indefinite extent; but if he would perceive the relation between these facts, which is truth in its high sense, he must make himself ardently passive (if we may use such a phrase) to the impress of that truth, hushing his own personality lest some prejudice should bias his conclusions. This principle is well recognized by Science in her

own domain. It is the scientific conscience, the faith that in one who is willing
to see the truth there is something so at-
tuned to, so made after the pattern of the
truth itself, that one will recognize and
receive the other. We may call this fac-
ulty by no higher names than candor and
sound judgment; but it is in reality nothing less than God in us recognizing and accepting the Infinite God, who will stand
revealed as such when both religious and
scientific thinkers extend the area of their
acceptance to take in all facts, physical and
spiritual, as belonging to one universal
life.

It requires much faith thus to see life
whole, to bring both classes of facts into
our field of vision at once, and see them
ruled by the same laws and bound together
by the same principles, because the balance
of human belief is still so heavy on the
material side. Even the most spiritual
lives accord to unseen realities a confidence

which differs widely from the easy unconscious reliance with which they handle
dress, food, and other practical problems.
This is not strange: we are just emerging
from matter; we have been surrounded
by material forms from our earliest years.
No wonder our life flows out to them. It
is not cause for blame, it is simply the fact.
But now, if instead of drawing a hard and
fast line between material and spiritual
things, so called, we can have faith enough
to try the experiment of accepting them
both together, the scientific conscience
will itself oblige us to transfer the centre
of our lives from self to God.

By the very act of opening ourselves to
spiritual truth we break down the narrow
limits of selfhood and become conscious of
the universal Life. The inflow of this life
fills us with a sense of harmony; and why?
Because being the universal life it holds all
things in right relation one to another, and
by virtue of that right relation, *when ac-*

cepted by us, tends to make whole or bring into order the individual and ultimately the race. We all recognize order as the arrangement of details in obedience to a central plan, so that one idea, one life, pervades the whole; conversely, it is only by being brought into such order that a mass of details becomes a whole, moved by one impulse. In proportion as man becomes individually whole (that is, orderly in his physical structure and working) and part of a greater whole (that is, in his right place and relation to all other beings which compose that whole), in that proportion he becomes conscious of the universal life whose laws produce this wholeness and order, and in its organic centre he recognizes God.

When this practical — not merely intellectual — recognition of God becomes the common experience, material things will grow transparent to the Spirit in ways that we cannot dream of now, but we may be

sure that they will " make all things new."
We need dread no catastrophes in those
days; they will be of the past. The vio-
lent wrenching from man of his material
possessions is only needed, only caused in
fact, by his clinging to them overmuch.
As a picture that we have outgrown is
first seldom looked at, then relegated to an
attic and at last to a dust-heap, so we shall
grow indifferent to, lay aside, and unconsciously leave behind our mortality and all
that belongs to it as we step forward to
better things. Thus death will be dissolved
in life.

The leaders in Mental Healing, like the
prophets of old, have seen this day from
afar, and are trying to bring its laws and
conditions into immediate effect for the
help of man. The results they have to
show are impressive, less by reason of their
extent—though this is considerable —than
by reason of their extraordinary harmoniz-
ing of man's physical with his spiritual

nature. This is what we should expect if the true divine order has been found, and the central force touched which moves all things together, both spiritual and physical.

Harm has been done in some cases because extremists in the new practice have not added patience and knowledge to their faith. In their eagerness to bring their idealism to bear they have ignored the actual, and have been unmindful of the supreme delicacy and difficulty of the task of adjusting details in that borderland where the ideal and the actual meet. Some unwise ones have insisted, for example, that an aged woman, dying of a terrible disease, should abandon all the palliatives that were making her last hours endurable, and trust herself wholly to faith in the hope of a cure. Speedy and suffering death ensued. The patient was too far gone; she had too slight a hold on the physical to make it possible for

her life to flow much longer through
its channels. The healers should have
recognized this, and realized that a course
which might safely and wisely be pre-
scribed for a person of average, though
disordered, vitality, may be ruinous if
applied to a case like the one we have
mentioned. The breath that fans a vigorous flame into greater activity may
suffice to extinguish a feeble one. Undoubtedly the woman might have been
cured by a miracle; but to achieve this,
the miracle-worker must have had wisdom
in proportion to his faith. Christ, the
great miracle-worker, *was himself* the
Truth, the Wisdom. We are only beginning to assimilate it.

Such abuse of the principles of Mental
Healing is sure to bring its own punish-
ment. In time, these blots on the record
of the new practice will disappear, and
men will own that it is doing a real service and is making a bold advance into

the very heart of Christianity, forcing it to yield its deepest secrets for the healing of the nations. Homœopathy has made a step in the same direction; it counsels the introduction of poisons in infinitesimal doses into the human system in the faith that the disorder they cause will rouse the inherent order or wholeness of the physical organism to assert its integrity by driving out the intruder and everything that resembles him. This is a spiritual advance of no small magnitude, because it acknowledges and relies on the reactive power of a Divine life-principle in man. But so long as homœopathy uses any material means at all, it hesitates on the brink of that absolute faith in the Divine life-principle which sees in it a first cause, active instead of reactive; and thus by supreme trust in it brings the vital power immediately to bear. Mental Healing has dared to do this, and should enjoy the credit due to its courage.

Blending the spiritual and physical in one life does not do away with duty, but transfigures duty by an ever-present sense of heavenly aid. When we practically treat the physical as included in the spiritual life, several things follow in our experience.

1. If God is in and of us, if His conception is the secret of our individuality, then that individuality may be trusted and revered. We may train and develop instead of suppressing it, and thereby "hitch our wagon to a star."

2. There is a star for each one of us, — an ideal perfection to be made actual by our acceptance. Armed with this certainty we can bring the ideal treatment to bear both on moral and physical perversity, — seeing through the evil manifestation, whether it be wilfulness or bodily pain, to the perfect wholeness that God's will holds for the erring one here and now. God's will is timeless. His perfec-

tion, and man's perfection in Him, is an eternal *present.* Time is only the delay of our wills in accepting, and space only the separation of our wills in existing apart from, that omnipresence, or all-presentness, of God.

3. When the two lives become one in our experience, we find that in obliterating the line between them we have struck a mighty blow at the fear of death; and that death has been a limit, a place of parting to us, only because we have, by maintaining this line, insisted upon making it so. In one sense death — the Cross — will always remain, because it is in its essence the passing from a lower truth to a higher one.[1] In this we shall ever rejoice, as those who have learned the true meaning of the Cross now rejoice to accept it and pass through it continually to larger life. But as the two worlds become

[1] Death is the supreme physical expression of this truth of the Cross.

more and more one to us, our common
assurance of the supreme reality of that
which is now unseen will remove all un-
certainty, all terror, from the step that
carries us from one world to the other.
We shall then see in death and the Cross
only a wide-open, sunny portal through
which all may throng joyously to seek
supplies of life.

Christ is the personal embodiment of
this future for man. He is the turning
from ourselves to God. No man ever
stepped forth out of himself to a higher
thought, but by that step he embodied
himself in the Christ. There is no other
way. Christ is part of the constitution
and course of Nature, the eternal movement from the human to the Divine.
Between our isolated, stunted selves and
the great ocean of God's life stands the
Cross. If we turn away, it looms terrible
with fear; if we press it joyfully to our
hearts, we pass through it to peace and

infinite life, and the crucified Christ becomes the crowned Christ for us. Standing then in Christ, our eyes open on the
vastness of God, and we see the ideal
beauty and glory of every created form.
No longer doubting, we grasp the ideal
for ourselves and for all about us, becoming in our measure the Christ for them
and revealing them to themselves.

But what of the historic Christ? Let
us think of Him as the personal manifestation of the universal Deity in relation
to this planet; the Soul of the whole
earth; the Eternal Word which embodied
God's thought of this world and its destinies. It was then all Christ from the
beginning, both the mass of matter, and
the possibilities of spiritual life to be
evolved therefrom. Christ, the soul of
mankind, was the forming principle, but
was not manifested or individualized; just
as when a child is born, his soul is the
principle which forms him and determines

his aspect and his destinies, and yet it is long before he comes to himself and learns to rule by his soul, and bring his body into subjection. So the world waited long, and the struggle was fierce, with here and there a piling up of monstrous evil, and here and there a foreshadowing of the spiritual birth to come, till the day dawned when out of the lowest came the highest, and from a manger the first perfect Man arose and reached to Heaven. Then the soul of mankind was freed, and the way opened to the Infinite.

If this was what happened when Christ was born, we should expect to see, as indeed we find, the Soul of mankind, Christ Jesus, leading a perfect life, in which spirit, for the first time triumphant over matter, could move it at will. It was a perfect life in its obedience to God, but it was a maimed life so far as the flesh was concerned; in other words, it was in-complete. Therefore it passed through the gates of death and became invisible to mortal eyes. But it has been growing ever since, and bringing human conditions more and more into harmony with itself. Centuries have been needed, and more may yet go by, before that life reaches its full growth and stature. Not till every human being realizes that he is part of the life of Christ, and that his fealty and that of all his fellows is the necessary condition of its completeness, will Christ return visibly to earth, shining from the east unto the west in the wide glory of a perfected humanity. In some hearts He already reigns supreme, and to their loyalty is granted a vision of the joyous time to come when physical science shall bring as her tribute such a thorough comprehension of material laws and conditions, that disease and accident shall be held at bay; when art and music shall scorn to paint and sing anything less than the higher harmonies; when every human being shall respect his own individuality as divine, and his body as a temple of the Holy Ghost, and yet shall be so conscious of his vital relation to all others in the great body of Christ, and so filled with loyal obedience to the Head, that his right shall never be allowed to work another's wrong. Then life shall flow in a full current through all the mighty form of the God-man, Christ Jesus.

This day may be very far off, but its coming is certain; and while we wait we work for it and welcome every helpful influence. If in the search for health man finds that the Spirit of God can and does move matter when its power is invoked in accordance with the high and holy conditions it imposes, then there will come to him an ever-increasing confidence in that Spirit, and great discoveries will be made about the working of its laws. They will become so well understood a science, that we shall depend on them as simply as we now depend on the law of gravitation, and we shall handle the Bread of Life with as much naturalness as we now handle the daily bread upon our tables. Then will Christ keep His ancient promise, and drink the wine of His life new with us in the kingdom of God.